MYSTERIES OF THE PLANETS

ALSO BY FRANKLYN M. BRANLEY

Mysteries of the Universe Series

Mysteries of Life on Earth and Beyond
Mysteries of Outer Space
Mysteries of the Satellites
Mysteries of the Universe

Black Holes, White Dwarfs, and Superstars
Columbia & Beyond
  The Story of the Space Shuttle
Comets, Meteoroids, and Asteroids
  Mavericks of the Solar System
The Earth: *Planet Number Three*
The Electromagnetic Spectrum
  Key to the Universe
Halley: Comet 1986
Jupiter
  King of the Gods, Giant of the Planets
Mars: *Planet Number Four*
The Milky Way: *Galaxy Number One*
The Moon: *Earth's Natural Satellite*
The Nine Planets
Saturn: *The Spectacular Planet*
Space Colony
  Frontier of the 21st Century
The Sun: *Star Number One*

MYSTERIES OF THE UNIVERSE SERIES

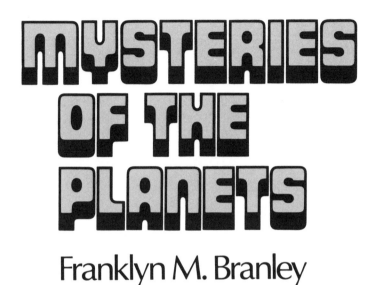

MYSTERIES OF THE PLANETS

Franklyn M. Branley

Diagrams by Sally J. Bensusen

LODESTAR BOOKS   E. P. DUTTON   NEW YORK

Jacket photo: Montage of Voyager 2 images shows the blue green Uranus overlaid with an artist's conception of the planet's dark rings as they might appear. A portion of a Voyager close-approach image of Miranda, the planet's nearest satellite, is arranged in the foreground. TERENCE MURTAGH, THE PLANETARIUM, ARMAGH, NORTHERN IRELAND

Photograph on opposite page
courtesy of NASA / Hayden Planetarium

Library of Congress Cataloging in Publication Data

Branley, Franklyn Mansfield.
  Mysteries of the planets.

  (Mysteries of the universe series)
  "Lodestar books."
  Bibliography: p.
  Includes index.
  Summary: Discusses the nine known planets of our solar system, their characteristics and movements, as well as the possibilities of other undiscovered planets and extraterrestrial life.
  1. Planets—Juvenile literature. [1. Planets]
I. Bensusen, Sally J., ill. II. Title. III. Series:
Branley, Franklyn Mansfield. Mysteries of the universe series.
QB602.B718   1987   523.4   87-20086
ISBN 0-525-67240-0

Published in the United States by E. P. Dutton,
2 Park Avenue, New York, N.Y. 10016,
a division of NAL Penguin Inc.

Published simultaneously in Canada by
Fitzhenry & Whiteside Limited, Toronto

Editor: Virginia Buckley

Printed in the U.S.A.   W   First Edition
10 9 8 7 6 5 4 3 2 1

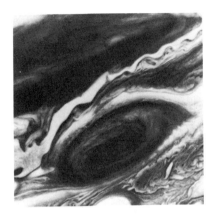

CONTENTS

MYSTERIES OF THE PLANETS

THE NUMBER OF PLANETS

How many planets are there?

We usually think that there are nine planets. In order of each one's distance from the Sun, they are Mercury, Venus, Earth, Mars, Jupiter, Saturn, Uranus, Pluto, and Neptune. In 1999, Pluto will become the most distant. But there may be more planets.

Planets move in elliptical orbits. Their motions are understood so well that astronomers can predict where a planet will be at any time in the future, as well as where it was located at any time in the past. But all planets do not always behave as expected. For example, Neptune was discovered because Uranus was not moving as predicted. It appeared that an object having considerable mass was affecting the motion of Uranus. Astronomers figured out how massive the object had to be and where it should be located. When telescopes were pointed at that location, Neptune was discovered.

A similar sequence of events occurred in this century. Uranus and Neptune moved in ways that implied there was a massive object out beyond them. When its position was suggested, astronomers took thousands of photos of that section of the sky. When the pictures were studied, a very dim object was seen to have changed location among the stars. In 1930, Clyde Tombaugh announced that the dim object was planet number nine. Later it was named Pluto. The name was suggested by Venetia Burney, now Mrs. Maxwell Phair, who at that time was eleven years old and very interested in astronomy. Venetia knew about the other planets, and she also knew a lot about mythology. She decided Pluto was the right name because he was the god of the underworld and supposedly wore a helmet that made him invisible. Pluto *is* invisible, except to powerful telescopes.

In following years when astronomers studied Pluto, they discovered that its mass was not great enough to strongly affect the movements of Neptune. It seems that there should be another massive object beyond Neptune, and beyond Pluto.

There are astronomers who still search for that elusive object. If they find it, it will become planet number ten. Is there such a planet out there? That is a mystery.

About a hundred years ago a topic of concern to many people was Vulcan. An observer had reported seeing a tiny object move across the disk of the Sun. It was not a known object, therefore many people believed it to be a planet in the space between Mercury and the Sun. If there were such a planet, it would be very hot. Thus it was named Vulcan, after the Roman god of fire.

Perhaps the person who reported the sighting was in error, for all attempts to see the planet have been unsuccessful. A favorite challenge for eclipse viewers was to attempt to see Vulcan at such times. If it were there, it might be visible during an eclipse because the region close to the Sun is then darkened.

An argument supporting the existence of Vulcan is the fact that Mercury's orbit changes more than it is supposed to. However, in 1905 when Albert Einstein presented his theory of relativity, astronomers were able to explain the changed orbit by applying the theory. Despite this, a few people still believe Vulcan exists and they continue to scan the region close to the Sun, hoping to glimpse it.

Why do the planets vary so much?

No matter what aspect you might consider, there are many differences among the planets.

They range in size from tiny Pluto, with a diameter of 3000 kilometers, to giant Jupiter, which is 142 830 kilometers across at the equator. Earth is midsized: Four of the planets are smaller than we are, and four are larger.

The planets also vary a great deal in mass, the amount of material they contain. For comparison, suppose we say that the mass of Earth is 1. Jupiter has 318 times more material. But it would take more than five hundred Plutos to equal a single Earth.

When we know mass and volume, or size, of a planet, we can find density, which tells us how close together the material is packed. As a base for measuring, we say that the density of water is 1—1 cubic centimeter of water weighs 1 gram. If we find that 1 cubic centimeter of soil weighs 4 grams, the soil has a density of 4.

Densities of the planets are found to range from 0.5 for Pluto and 0.69 for Saturn to 5.52 for Earth—the most dense of all the planets. Pluto and Saturn have densities less than that of water. They must be made of gases or ice. (The density of ice is less than 1.) We know that Earth contains a great deal of solid rock, which is material of high density. When calculated with the water and gases of the planet, overall density becomes 5.52.

Mercury and Mars lack significant atmospheres, as does Pluto. The surface of Mercury is covered with craters, which were probably formed billions of years ago and have not been filled in and smoothed off. It does not have enough gravity to hold an atmosphere. Likewise, the gravity of Mars is not very great, although the planet does retain some carbon dioxide, which is a heavy gas.

The atmosphere of Venus is mostly carbon dioxide. Lighter gases have escaped from the planet, and the carbon dioxide has become more and more concentrated. Tiny Pluto has

INFORMATION ABOUT THE PLANETS

	Distance from Sun (million km)	Revolution Time	Velocity in Orbit (km per sec)	Rotation Time	Diameter at Equator (km)
Mercury	57.8	88.00 d	47.5	58.65 d	4868
Venus	108.2	224.70 d	34.9	244.00 d	12 122
Earth	149.6	365.26 d	29.6	23h 56m	12 757
Mars	227.9	687.00 d	24.0	24h 37m	6787
Jupiter	778.3	11.86 y	12.9	9h 56m	142 830
Saturn	1429.9	29.46 y	9.6	10h 14m	119 330
Uranus	2869.6	84.01 y	6.7	17h 24m	50 800
Neptune	4496.6	164.80 y	5.4	16h 00m	49 500
Pluto	5911.7	247.70 y	4.7	6.40 d	3000

very low gravity, not nearly enough to hold an atmosphere.

The major planets—Jupiter, Saturn, Uranus, and Neptune—are all gaseous. They may have solid cores. If so, these cores are very small relative to the sizes of the planets. The outer gases of these big planets are light, mainly hydrogen. In the interior sections, heavier gases such as ammonia and methane are packed together tightly. They are compressed enough to become liquid

Key
d days   m minutes
h hours   y years

Mass	Density	Volume	Surface Gravity	Atmosphere (main gases)	Temperature (°Celsius)	Satellites
0.05	5.50	0.06	0.38	Xe, Ar	349	0
0.80	5.23	0.88	0.90	CO_2	460	0
1.00	5.52	1.00	1.00	N_2, O_2	14	1
0.11	3.93	0.15	0.38	CO_2	−68 to +28	2
18.00	1.33	1318.00	2.64	H_2, He	−120	16 (?)
95.20	0.69	736.00	1.13	H_2, He	−156	17 (?)
14.60	1.56	62.00	1.07	H_2, He	−200	15 (?)
17.30	1.54	57.00	1.08	H_2, He	−200	2 (?)
0.0019	0.50	0.018	0.30	None (?)	−225	1

or even solid—density increases toward the center of each.

Many of the differences among the planets are related to differences in mass, density, and gravity. Also, distances from the Sun strongly affect the planets. While astronomers can explain many of the conditions of the planets, they are far from understanding all about them. Each of the planets holds mysteries that astronomers continue to explore.

Why are there nine planets?

Very likely planets and stars form when gigantic gaseous clouds pack together. The greatest amounts of material would become stars, and lesser amounts would become planets. If this is so, the number of planets would depend somewhat on the mass of the original cloud. Other factors include the mass of the central star, the rate of packing, and the size of the individual particles. There appears to be no particular reason why our system is made of nine planets. Other planetary systems, if they exist—and we have reason to believe they do, might contain more or less than nine. Indeed, while many stars may be the centers of planetary systems, others may be members of star systems consisting of two or three or more stars going around one another. In such cases, masses were great enough for the objects to become stars rather than planets. (Stars are more massive than planets.) In addition, there are a good many solitary stars—single stars that are not associated with a star system or with a planet system.

Are there planets outside the solar system?

Our solar system—which is made up of the Sun and planets, satellites, comets, planetary rings, asteroids, and interplanetary dust—is an extremely small part of the universe. Many people believe there must be other planetary systems contained in the vastness of the universe. Evidence that they may be right is mounting.

Satellites that are sensitive to infrared, or heat, radiation have detected clouds of particles that are cool relative to stars in the vicinity of Vega, as well as several other stars. These clouds may be made of particles that are presently joining together to form planets. Since the particles are very small, we may be seeing a very early stage in planet formation.

Ground-based telescopes have revealed a disk of solid material surrounding Beta Pictoris—this is a star in the southern constellation of Pictor, the painter's easel. There are breaks in the

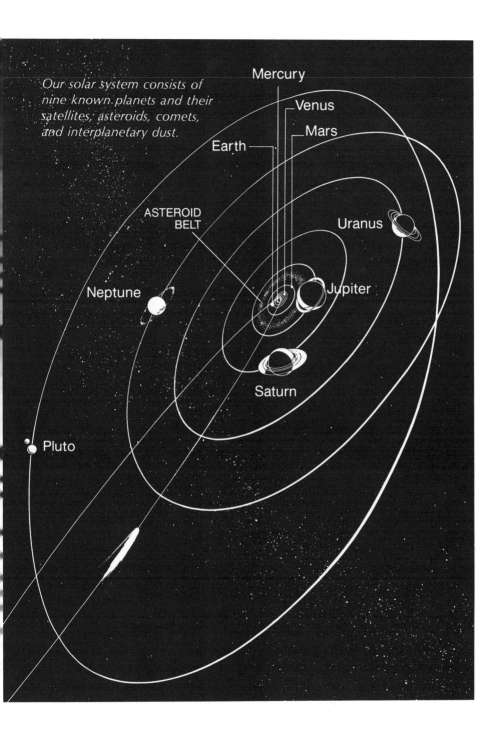

Our solar system consists of
nine known planets and their
satellites, asteroids, comets,
and interplanetary dust.

Mercury

Venus

Mars

Earth

ASTEROID
BELT

Uranus

Neptune

Jupiter

Saturn

Pluto

disk, and it has been suggested that these may be locations where small particles have already packed together to produce larger masses. Here we may be witnessing a later stage in the evolution of planets.

In 1984, other telescopes designed to pick up infrared radiation detected what may be a planet going around Van Biesbroeck 8, also called VB8, a star that is some 21 light-years away. It is in the constellation Ophiuchus, the serpent bearer, a huge formation that lies north and east of Scorpius. The object moving around Van Biesbroeck 8, which was named after the astronomer Peter Van Biesbroeck, is a large sphere of gases about nine-tenths the size of Jupiter but at least thirty times more dense.

If it is a planet, it appears to be much different from those in our solar system. Because of the high mass, many believe it is more likely a peculiar type of star called a brown dwarf. It may lack enough mass and interior temperature to develop nuclear reactions and thus produce intense light energy, yet be too massive to be classified as a planet. This remains a fascinating mystery to be explored.

There may be untold numbers of planets in our own galaxy. Beyond us, there may be endless numbers in the galaxies that abound in the universe. The search for them remains a challenge.

MOTIONS OF THE PLANETS

How do planets revolve and rotate?

Earth moves in many different ways. We are not aware of any of the motions, although we experience their effects. For example, we have day and night because of Earth's rotation, and a principal cause of seasonal changes is our revolution around the Sun.

At the equator the speed of our rotation is 1600 kilometers an hour. As one moves toward the poles, the speed of rotation decreases. At the same time, we are moving around the Sun at a speed of 29.6 kilometers a second—over 100 000 kilometers an hour.

At 1600 kilometers an hour, we complete a rotation in 23 hours, 56 minutes. Mercury, Venus, and Pluto each take several days to rotate, while all the other planets rotate in only a few hours. All the planets except Venus rotate in the same direction, from west to east. Venus rotates from east to west. From the surface of Venus, the Sun would rise in the west and set in the east. However, no one would be able to see it because of the heavy clouds in the atmosphere.

Exactly why Venus moves in this fashion remains unexplained. Perhaps it is because of strong tidal effects produced by the nearness of the Sun. During its early history, Venus may have had extensive oceans. There would have been very high tides, and the drag of the water could have altered the planet's motions. While Mercury is closer to the Sun, it would not have had such extreme tides and drag, for it probably never had an ocean. The backward motion of Venus is another mystery yet to be solved.

Earth takes one year to go around the Sun—to revolve. Mercury, closest to the Sun of all the planets, has the shortest year—only 88 days. The length of the year becomes greater with increasing distance from the Sun. Pluto's year is 247.7 Earth years. The revolution speed of each planet is just enough to hold it in orbit. The closer it is to the Sun, the faster it must move. For a similar reason, the speeds of artificial satellites decrease with distance. Nearby ones that are about 450 kilometers away go some 27 000 kilometers an hour. Those at 35 000 kilometers move more slowly. If an artificial satellite were 382 000 kilometers away, the distance of the Moon, it would revolve around Earth at only 3600 kilometers an hour.

How does the solar system move?

All parts of the solar system are in motion. In fact, all parts of the entire universe are moving.

More than 99 percent of the mass of the solar system is in the Sun. Therefore, the Sun has strong gravity, and whatever the Sun does affects all of the solar system.

The Sun rotates, and it also travels through space. It is moving 20 kilometers a second and traveling toward the constellation Hercules. As the Sun moves, it carries Earth and the rest of the solar system along with it.

So, while we are rotating 1600 kilometers an hour and going around the Sun at 29 kilometers a second, we are also speeding toward Hercules at 20 kilometers a second. But that is not all; there are other motions.

Earth is in the Milky Way galaxy, and the entire galaxy is rotating. It goes around once in 250 million years. That movement must also be added to all the others.

Earth is rotating, revolving around the Sun, and moving through space toward Hercules. The solar system makes one turn around the galaxy every 250 million years. The entire galaxy is moving through space.

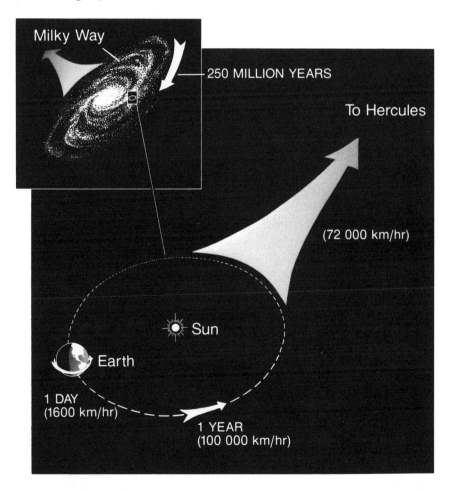

Milky Way

250 MILLION YEARS

To Hercules

(72 000 km/hr)

Sun

Earth

1 DAY
(1600 km/hr)

1 YEAR
(100 000 km/hr)

In addition to rotating, the galaxy moves through space. The Milky Way is one of about twenty galaxies that form what is called the local group. And all of those galaxies move around one another.

Will the planets continue to move?

We would expect so, for once a body is moving it continues to move because there is nothing to stop it. So as long as the planets exist, they will move. But they will not exist forever.

That is because the Sun is not everlasting. It is believed that the Sun is 5 billion years old, halfway through its lifetime of 10 billion years. Eventually it will become a much smaller and cooler star. Before it does, the Sun will expand. It may become so large that it will surround Earth and reach almost to Mars. When that happens, Earth will get very hot—hot enough for all of it to be changed to gases. We will become part of the Sun itself. However, this expansion is not likely to occur for several billion years.

MAGNETISM OF THE PLANETS

Earth acts like a magnet. We know this because on Earth a compass needle lines up in a north/south direction. It would not do so on Venus or Mars, for neither of those planets has a magnetic field. Why they do not is a mystery.

Why is Earth magnetic?

Earth has magnetism because of something called the dynamo effect. The planet rotates fairly rapidly. Inside Earth there is a molten layer that rotates at a different rate from the solid portion of the planet. The molten layer, which contains metal, is an electric conductor. As the conductor moves, a magnetic field is produced. The electric conductor moving through a magnetic field produces electricity. In turn the electricity produces magnetism, and so the two feed each other. The planet is electrical and it is magnetic.

Why do Venus and Mars lack magnetism?

When space probes went to Venus and Mars, they found magnetic fields, but these fields were very weak and irregular. Scien-

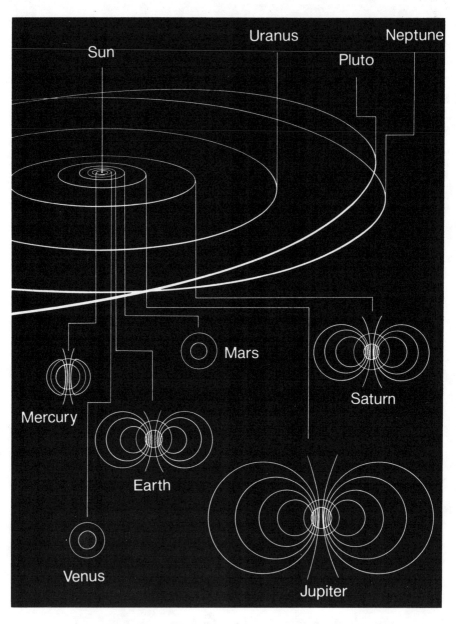

The magnetism of the planets results from what is called the dynamo effect—variable rotations of planetary layers or convection currents, up-and-down motions, of semi-molten materials.

tists are quite certain that the fields are not produced on the planets, but are reflections of the Sun's magnetic field.

Venus is about the size of Earth, so it is often called our sister planet. However, the planet rotates very slowly, taking 224 days to complete a single turn. It is believed that in order for the dynamo effect to occur, a planet must spin faster than that, or there must be up-and-down movements, or convection currents, of the molten material inside. Apparently there are no such movements inside Venus, certainly not enough to produce a measurable amount of magnetism.

Mars is almost half the size of Earth. Its rotation period is 24 hours, 37 minutes, which should be fast enough to generate a magnetic field. But it does not have one, and that is puzzling. The density of the planet, the compactness of its material, is low. It is so low that the planet must either have a very small metallic core—metals have high density—or no core at all. Perhaps there is a small metal core, and a weak field is generated deep within the planet—a field that is not strong enough to register on instruments placed on the surface.

Is Pluto magnetic?

We do not know, but it would be a great surprise if the planet turned out to have a magnetic field. It is the smallest of all the planets, and its density is low—the lowest of all. Also, the planet rotates very slowly, making a turn in a little more than 6 days. It seems that tiny Pluto has none of the conditions needed for the generation of magnetism.

Why is Mercury's magnetism unusual?

Mercury has a magnetic field, although it is very weak, only about a thousandth as strong as ours. But according to the dynamo theory, it should have none at all. This is another unsolved riddle.

Mercury is a small planet, 4868 kilometers across. (The diameter of Earth, you remember, is 12 757 kilometers.) Mercury rotates slowly, having a rotation period of almost 59 days. It moves so slowly that the discovery of even a small amount of magnetism was a surprise. Maybe the reason for the magnetism is the planet's density. It is high, about the same as Earth's. Such high density implies a rather large metallic core. Scientists believe that there are up-and-down movements of the molten material in this core. So although Mercury's rotation is slow, these vertical movements would provide the energy required for the dynamo effect to operate.

Why do gaseous planets have magnetic fields?

The gaseous planets—Jupiter, Saturn, Uranus, and probably Neptune—do have magnetic fields. They all rotate rapidly: Jupiter and Saturn in about 10 hours, Uranus in 17½, and Neptune in 16. The densities of all of them are low, but all are very massive. Hydrogen and helium have been packed together so tightly that they behave like metals, and thus are electric conductors. The planets have layers, and the layers rotate at different speeds, producing the dynamo effect.

Spacecraft carrying magnetometers, instruments that measure magnetism, have flown by Jupiter, Saturn, and Uranus and have found magnetic fields. When they probe the region around Neptune, it is very likely that another planet will be added to the list of those that generate magnetic fields.

TEMPERATURES OF THE PLANETS

The Sun gives off a tremendous amount of energy, and sends it out in all directions. At our distance from the Sun, Earth receives only one two-billionth of the energy that the Sun produces. It is a tiny fraction of the total, yet it is enough to supply us with all the energy that we need and to keep the planet at 14° Celsius (C).

While the part of Earth that is in sunlight is receiving energy, the other half of the planet is losing energy. The amounts balance each other, so while day and night temperatures vary, the temperature of Earth as a whole remains the same year in and year out. A small part of Earth's heat comes from radioactive atoms. This amount decreases with time because the atoms become less radioactive, causing a slight but continuous cooling of the planet.

How are Jupiter and Saturn heated?

In some ways temperature conditions on Jupiter and Saturn are the same as on Earth. Just as we receive energy from the Sun, so also do these giant planets. They are bigger than Earth is and have much more surface area for absorbing energy. But they are much farther from the Sun. By the time solar radiation reaches these planets, it does not contain as much energy. Still, enough remains

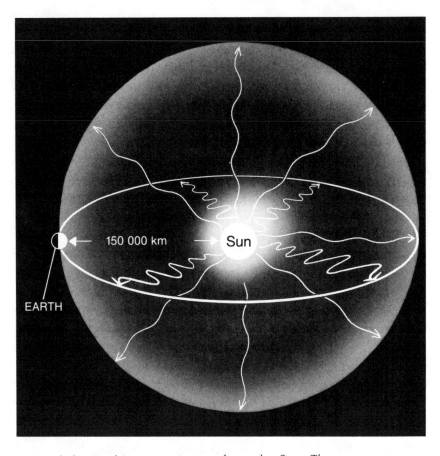

Most of the Earth's energy comes from the Sun. The energy radiates in all directions. It is as if the Sun is at the center of a ball with a radius of 150 million kilometers. Earth occupies one two-billionths of the surface of that ball—we receive one two-billionth of the energy the Sun radiates.

to keep temperatures considerably above absolute zero, which is −273°C.

The interior temperatures of Jupiter and Saturn appear to be much higher, perhaps reaching several thousand degrees. They are so high that solar energy could not be the source. There has to be some other explanation. Jupiter and Saturn give off more energy than they receive. This means that somehow these planets are generating heat.

Some people suggest this is original heat that formed some 4.6 billion years ago, when the planets came into existence. This means the planets are still cooling down. Others believe that the planets contain large amounts of radioactive atoms that give off energy, much of it in the form of heat. Eventually these atoms will lose their radioactivity, and the amount of heat given off by the planets will drop. According to others, heat may be generated in the atmosphere. Solid crystals may rain down through the gases, causing friction which may produce heat.

Some of these same theories may also explain the temperature conditions on Uranus and Neptune, the other two gaseous giants.

Why do the Moon and Mercury have such extreme temperatures?

Like Earth, Mercury has a day/night temperature change. But unlike Earth, the day temperature of Mercury is a blistering 349°C, and the night temperature drops to 185°C below zero. The Moon also has extremes, though not as great. When sunlight falls there, temperatures soar to 132°C; on the dark half of the Moon, temperatures drop to −156°C.

Both the Moon and Mercury lack atmospheres. Just as a blanket holds in body heat, a planet's atmosphere holds in the heat of the planet. When there is no atmosphere, there is no way of retaining heat, so an object cools rapidly. Earth's atmosphere is sufficient to slow down heat loss. Although Earth cools at night, there is only a slight drop in temperature.

Why is Venus the hottest planet?

There is very little loss of heat from Venus, much less than there is from Earth. The temperature of Venus remains just about the same both day and night, staying at 460°C, higher than any of the other planets or their satellites. Most of the atmosphere of Venus is carbon dioxide. Why the temperature of Venus is so high remains a mystery, although the dense atmosphere is probably the main cause.

The most widely accepted theory formulated to explain the high temperature is the greenhouse, or blanket, idea. Radiation comes from the Sun in shortwaves that can pass through the glass of a greenhouse. When these shortwaves strike other materials, they are changed to longer waves. These long waves cannot pass through glass, and so they are trapped inside the greenhouse. This is known as the greenhouse effect. When you stand in front of a sunny window on a cold day, you can feel it. Radiation energy passes through the cold winter air and through the glass. When it falls on you the energy becomes heat, so you feel warm.

Carbon dioxide acts very much like glass in the way it handles radiation. Shortwaves can pass through it, but long waves cannot.

Shortwave radiation passes through the glass, into the greenhouse, where it is converted to long-wave radiation, which cannot readily move back through the glass. Thus heat builds up in the greenhouse. Similarly, the atmosphere of Venus allows shortwave radiation from the Sun to enter but does not allow the resulting long-wave radiation, heat, to escape.

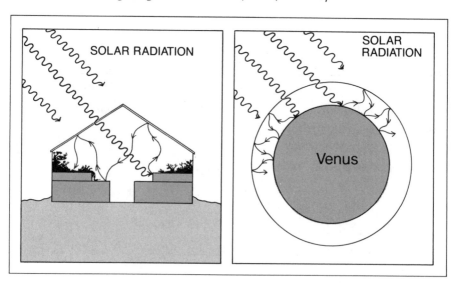

On Venus, radiation from the Sun passes through the atmosphere. It is changed to heat, which cannot move back through the carbon dioxide, so it is trapped. During a Venusian day, heat builds up. But very little is lost during a night on the planet—the temperature holds steady at 460°C.

The heat on Venus is destructive. It makes the surface into a barren wasteland. Space probes that landed there were rapidly destroyed by the high temperature and by the high pressure, which is a hundred times greater than the pressure on Earth. Here the pressure is 14 pounds on a square inch; on Venus the pressure is more than a half ton on each square inch.

Venus is a planet of many mysteries, not the least of which is its temperature. Perhaps the greenhouse explanation is the correct solution. It seems the most reasonable one to many people.

Why do parts of Mars heat up?

Regions of Mars may be very warm, up to 28°C, while other areas may be almost a hundred degrees cooler. Part of the explanation is related to atmosphere. The density of Mars' atmosphere is very low, so the greenhouse effect is not great. There is a rapid buildup of temperature and also a rapid cooling down.

Also, because of the tilt of Mars' axis, parts of the planet are exposed to direct rays of the Sun; that is, radiation comes in at a 90-degree angle to the surface. When that occurs, a large part of the radiation is absorbed. Where the radiation comes in at a slant, much of it glances off the surface. It is not absorbed and the region does not heat up.

Where the Sun is overhead, the temperature is high. And where the Sun is nearer the horizon, the temperature is considerably lower.

The same condition exists on Earth because its axis is tilted at about the same angle as the axis of Mars. However, Earth has a much denser atmosphere, which reduces heat loss, leading to a temperature range less extreme than that on Mars.

THE RINGS
OF THE PLANETS

The Italian scientist Galileo was one of the first people who experimented in order to find answers to his questions, and he was the first person to observe the sky using a telescope. He made several telescopes, and many were good enough for him to see slight bulges on either side of Saturn. He was at a loss to explain them. Later on, using better telescopes, he could see that the bulges were separated from the planet; they were rings. What a wonder that first sight must have been! Why should a planet have rings?

In the years between 1979 and 1981, two Voyager probes made close approaches to Jupiter, Saturn, and Uranus, as well as to many of the outer satellites. These approaches revealed that Saturn has perhaps thousands of rings.

Why do some planets have rings?

Saturn has many satellites. Long ago it may have had even more, some of which could have shattered into small pieces and formed a cloud. The pieces in the cloud could have banged into one another, lost energy, and eventually spread into a flat disk or ring.

According to Edouard Roche, a French astronomer of the

Neptune

Uranus

Saturn

Jupiter

Saturn, Jupiter, Uranus, and perhaps Neptune have rings. Observations appear to indicate that there are breaks in the rings. If so, we may be seeing strings of small, separate satellites. **25**

nineteenth century, a satellite will break apart if it moves within 2.4 times the radius of its planet. At that distance, the gravitational attraction of the planet becomes strong enough to raise huge bulges on the satellite. The satellite becomes so deformed that it shatters. Perhaps some of Saturn's satellites and the satellites of other planets had such a history. Or the rings of Jupiter and Uranus may have had a different history.

Disks or ring formations also occur elsewhere in the universe. The entire solar system is disk-shaped—it formed from a cloud of particles that at one time surrounded the Sun. Our galaxy is disk-shaped. It is likely that it formed from a much greater cloud and gradually assumed its present shape.

Rings are made of separate particles that are in many cases much smaller than grains of sand. But Saturn's rings contain some chunks as large as 10 or more meters across, and many others that are 3 to 5 meters in diameter. They appear to be largely chunks of ice with iron and stone mixed in.

What makes Saturn's rings?

Perhaps the rings are the remains of shattered satellites. But there may be another explanation.

Saturn's rings are made up largely of icy material, much the same as the particles that are thought to make up the cores of comets. According to the shattered-satellite theory, the outer regions of the solar system—the regions beyond Mars—used to swarm with chunks of rock and ice, many of them several kilometers in diameter. Occasionally these chunks were pulled into the orbits of Jupiter, Saturn, Uranus, and Neptune. Most of them captured by Saturn because of its location in the swarm.

Other chunks escaped. They were moving rapidly enough to have fought gravitation and to have left the solar system some 3.5 billion years ago. They would have joined a vast cloud of ice and rock particles that surrounds the solar system and is located about one-tenth of a light-year away. It is called the Oort cloud, after

Saturn is surrounded by hundreds, perhaps thousands, of rings. Many are made of very small particles. Small moons are embedded in some of the rings.   NASA / HAYDEN PLANETARIUM

the Dutch astronomer who suggested that such a cloud exists. The Oort cloud is believed to be the birthplace of comets.

Satellites may also have shattered because of collisions. The planets may have had many more large satellites than now exist. The satellites could have been large enough for the matter inside them to separate, with the more dense materials going to the center and the less dense matter forming in layers above it. These large satellites may have been struck by objects a hundred or so kilometers across, and both would have shattered. The small particles that remained would have joined together to make smaller satellites. Also, many of the particles would have remained disconnected. These may be the particles that now make up the rings.

The ice and rock particles were concentrated in the outer solar system, in the region around Saturn. Therefore we would expect that Saturn, with its strong gravity, would have the most dense ring system, and it does. For the same reason, we would expect Jupiter's ring system to be more sparse—and it is.

How is Jupiter's ring different from Saturn's?

Jupiter's single ring is different from Saturn's in that it contains a large amount of sulfur. It seems to be made of fine, smokelike sulfur dust, and less ice and rock.

There are many active volcanoes on Io, which is one of Jupiter's satellites. At least a dozen have been sighted since the first one was discovered. The volcanoes throw sulfur high above the surface of the satellite. Most of the sulfur settles down to the surface, but some escapes and is pulled toward Jupiter by the planet's strong gravitational field. Over the years, the captured dust has settled into a ring formation.

What did Voyager tell us about Uranus?

In January 1986, Voyager 2 flew within 80 000 kilometers of Uranus. During that approach we learned that the planet has at least fifteen satellites and at least eleven rings.

The planet probably has a small rocky core or central region that is surrounded by a superdense atmosphere. This atmosphere is made mostly of water; above that there is ammonia and methane. Above the dense atmosphere there seems to be a less dense region made of a mixture of hydrogen, methane, and a little helium and neon.

There appear to be cloud systems on the planet, and these clouds enable astronomers to measure prevailing winds. They seem to blow very fast and from east to west.

Uranus is a cold planet; for one thing, it is far from the Sun. Also, it has lost most of its internal heat. When it was formed, the materials that make up Uranus were very hot, just as were those that make up Earth. Presently only about 0.01 percent of our heat comes from the heat of formation. On Uranus perhaps 30 percent of its heat is from that source. Almost 70 percent of Jupiter's heat comes from inside the planet.

Uranus has a magnetic field, and it has a magnetosphere—a region that contains charged particles which are held together by magnetism. The magnetosphere is compressed on the Sun side of the planet. On the side away from the Sun, it is huge, extending some half a million kilometers into space.

Strangely, the magnetic poles are tilted some 60 degrees from the geographic poles. On our planet the magnetic poles are tilted about 11 degrees. Why there should be such a large tilt on Uranus remains a mystery.

The temperature of certain regions of Uranus is also a mystery. Because the axis is tilted so much, one pole remains in sunlight for several years, while the opposite one is in darkness. One would expect the pole in sunlight to be quite warm and the one in darkness to be cold. But that is not so. At both poles and at the equator, the temperature is about −200°C. Perhaps the dark pole is warmed by heat escaping from the interior. If so, why is the equator so warm—as warm as the poles? This is a puzzler.

Perhaps the biggest puzzle of all is that Uranus spins on its side. Our axis is tilted 23½ degrees, but the axis of Uranus is tilted 98 degrees. Perhaps long ago a planet-sized mass of material, perhaps as large as Earth, crashed into Uranus. The impact could have been enough to knock the planet onto its side. Maybe so, but no one really knows.

Uranus has many mysteries. It seems that whenever we make discoveries about a planet, new and different mysteries appear. That's the way it should be, for if we knew all the answers about Uranus, or any other planet, there would be nothing left to learn.

Are there rings around Neptune?

So far as we have observed, the answer has to be no. However, in the early 1980s an astronomer, Edward Guinan, discovered what might have been an effect of rings—the dimming of starlight. But other observers were unable to verify that rings existed.

A few years later, in 1984, some astronomers observed the dimming of a star as Neptune moved in front of it, apparently caused by a ring, or rings, around the planet. Their findings indicated that the ring is 10 to 15 kilometers wide and about 80 000 kilometers from the center of the planet. However, no dimming was seen on the other side of the planet, and so another mystery develops. Perhaps they saw part of a ring. But how could that be? Instead of rings, Neptune may have a string of small satellites that becomes visible only under certain rare conditions that are not presently understood.

If there should be one or several rings around Neptune it would not be surprising, since each of the other gaseous planets has rings.

As we learn more about the rings of Jupiter, Saturn, Uranus, and perhaps Neptune—what they are made of and how the particles move—entirely different theories may be needed to solve their many mysteries.

THE GREAT RED SPOT OF JUPITER

How large are Jupiter's storms?

The most violent big storms on Earth are hurricanes. They may be a thousand miles across. Winds in them blow at least 120 kilometers an hour, and they carry heavy rainfall. Hundreds of people have lost their lives in hurricanes, and towns and villages have been destroyed.

Fearsome as they are, hurricanes are mild compared to the storms that occur on Jupiter. One of the largest is located in the southern half of the planet, about 20 degrees south of the equator, in a region called the Great Red Spot. Two Earths, side by side, would just about cover the area encompassed by the spot.

The spot was first reported in 1664 by Robert Hooke, an English scientist, and for a time it was called Hooke's Spot. After that sighting, other observers saw the spot. But none of them realized that they all were looking at the same spot, one that persisted. It was believed that each observer was looking at something temporary and similar to the other changing formations of Jupiter.

That belief changed in 1878 when Ernst W. Tempel, a German astronomer, described the region carefully and gave its exact location. Since that time, the region has been called the Great

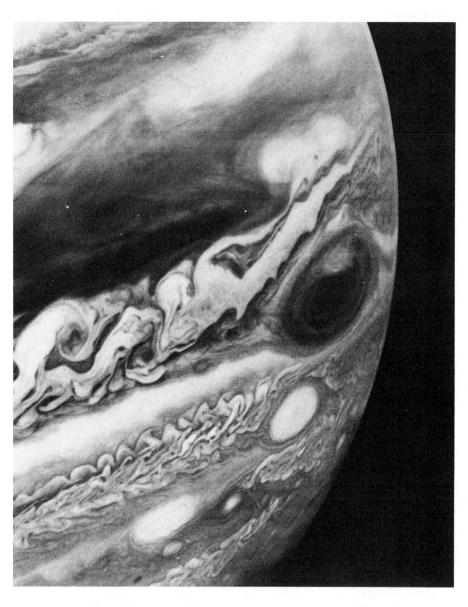

Bands of clouds extend around Jupiter. Here and there we can see dark and light areas where storms have developed. An especially large one is the Great Red Spot, shown in the center, at right. NASA / HAYDEN PLANETARIUM

Red Spot, and scientists have been challenged to explain it. Earth-based hurricanes are short-lived, lasting a few days at the most. But this storm on Jupiter has been studied for a hundred years, and it was first seen 300 years ago. To help their understanding of it, observers had to study Jupiter's atmosphere.

What makes up the atmosphere of Jupiter?

Unlike Earth, which is solid, Jupiter is a huge, gaseous planet, so large that 1300 Earths could fit inside it. The gases that make up Jupiter are hydrogen and helium, as well as smaller amounts of methane, ammonia, water vapor, and sulfur. At the top of the atmosphere, temperature is −130°C. Moving inward, the temperature soon soars to 1000°C and may reach 25 000° to 30 000°C deeper inside.

Pressure deep below the surface is so high that the hydrogen molecules are pushed together enough for them to become a liquid. Jupiter probably contains an ocean of hydrogen that lies below a dense atmosphere of hydrogen gas, helium, frozen ammonia, and methane. Deeper down, the hydrogen is so compressed that it behaves like a metal. For example, it conducts electricity, as was mentioned in Chapter 3. Toward the center of the planet there may be a core of rocky metallic materials not much larger than Earth. Or there may be no solid surface anywhere on Jupiter.

How do winds develop?

On Earth, storms break up as they move over differing formations. Forests, mountains, lakes, and cities interrupt the flow of winds and so cause them to blow out. Because Jupiter contains no mountains or valleys, there is nothing to break up storms. Once a movement of gases is started, the motion continues.

Jupiter's weather does not change from day to day as Earth's does. Once a wind system starts moving, it may remain established for centuries. For example, obvious formations on Jupiter are the colored belts that go around the planet. These are streams of winds. Clouds in them are produced by various concentrations of ammonia crystals and frozen methane.

Jupiter spins very fast. Its speed of rotation is 40 000 kilometers an hour along the equator. (Earth turns at a speed of about 1600 kilometers an hour.) This rapid rotation sets up movements of gases, and winds race along at hundreds of kilometers an hour. But all do not move in the same direction. For example, the belt of winds just below the Great Red Spot speeds west to east, while the winds just north of it blow in the opposite direction. They move unevenly around the spot, and swirls and eddies build up. For some time it was believed that these eddies produced movements of gases in the spot. But now the opposite seems to be

Tremendous swells and eddies have developed in the cloud bands of Jupiter. Around the spot, winds blow up to 500 kilometers an hour. The swirls may be extensive storm systems that drift.
NASA / HAYDEN PLANETARIUM

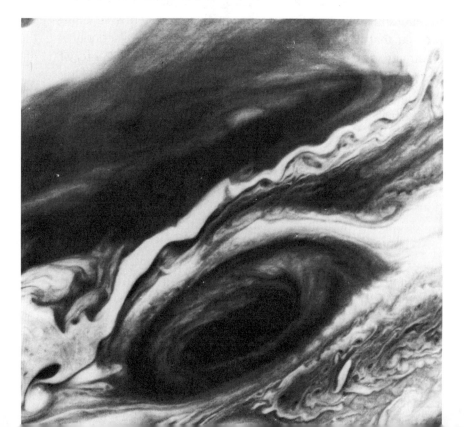

true—movement of gases in the spot provides energy that drives the winds.

Bands of clouds move around Jupiter, but gases in the spot rotate as a separate system. They make a turn once in six Earth days. Energy that keeps the gases moving comes from the interior of Jupiter.

The Sun supplies energy to all the planets, including Jupiter. But, as you know, Jupiter also produces energy. The interior of the planet must be very hot. Much of the heat comes from packing of the gases, and some from radioactive atoms, as we mentioned earlier. Also, part of Jupiter's heat may come from helium rain.

Helium condenses into drops that fall down, moving into and through the liquid hydrogen. Heat is released as the drops of helium rub against the fluid hydrogen. It is expected that heat from helium rain will increase as Jupiter's radioactive atoms become less energetic.

Heat from the interior of the planet is carried toward the surface in currents that move upward rapidly. Rotation of the planet causes the currents to be deflected into circular movements. They reach spinning speeds of several thousand kilometers an hour. There are no obstructions to interrupt the flow, so it has continued down through the centuries. As long as the interior heat is available to produce these currents, the gases will swirl about and the Great Red Spot will persist.

Could Jupiter become a star?

Jupiter is a massive planet. It contains 318 times the mass of Earth. Two-thirds of the material in all the planets and satellites, comets, and asteroids of the solar system is in Jupiter. Because it contains so much material, considerable heat is generated as gravitation packs the material together. If Jupiter were about ten times more massive than it is, the planet would be a star. That means the temperature produced would reach 10 000 000°C at the center, high enough for nuclear fusion to start. Hydrogen would be converted into helium, and tremendous heat would be released, which is what happens in a star.

A few astronomers have suggested that eventually Jupiter may become a star. The planet has a strong gravitational field, perhaps strong enough to pull in enough comets and asteroids to increase its mass to that of a star. Asteroids in orbit between Mars and Jupiter may collide or otherwise be thrown out of orbit and come under the influence of Jupiter. They may crash through the upper atmosphere and into the hydrogen ocean.

There are also billions of tons of cometary material in the Oort cloud. The chunks of ice, stone, and metal that make it up move in orbits around the solar system. On rare occasions, distant stars may move in close enough to exert a strong pull on these chunks, yanking a few out of orbit. Then they may come under the control of Jupiter's gravitation. Some of them may escape and go into a flat orbit, causing them to sweep close to and around the Sun. These would be the comets that are seen from time to time. Other chunks might be pulled into Jupiter, adding to its mass. Over millenniums, the mass so collected might become sufficient to cause the interior temperature to reach the level needed for nuclear fusion to begin. Then Jupiter would become a star.

It would take billions of years for this to happen, probably long after people have disappeared from Earth, or even after Earth has ceased to exist. And this is fortunate, because if Jupiter were to become a star, the additional heat we would receive could be enough to consume us. Either way, Earth will eventually disappear as a planet—it will be consumed by the Sun or by the Sun and the Jupiter star together.

No one can say whether or not Jupiter will ever become a star. It is a big question mark, as is the Great Red Spot. Although it has been observed for centuries, the spot remains a major mystery of the solar system.

7 THE WATERWAYS OF MARS

Is there life on Mars?

Back in the 1960s there were scientists who hoped that astronauts would find some signs of life when they landed on the Moon. No one expected that there would be sizable plants or animals, or even living microbes. But many suspected that if life had once existed there, clues would be discovered on the surface, or as fossils in Moon rocks. But no signs of any kind of life were found anywhere. The Moon is a dead, airless, waterless world, one that has never supported any living organism.

Though they had hoped to find life, most scientists did not truly believe they would. So, although they were disappointed, they were not surprised. They knew enough about the Moon to believe that life would have had a hard time starting there, or surviving once it had started.

Mars was another matter. Parts of the planet were warm enough to support life, some water was known to exist there, and very likely its present thin atmosphere had been much more dense at some time in the past. Therefore, Mars became the next location that scientists hoped to explore with probes to find out if any kind of life existed there.

Photographs, such as the one on page 39, were encouraging.

A person need not be an expert to see that the wiggly formations are waterways. They are channels along which large amounts of water have flowed. As far as we know, water is essential to the existence of life. There is no question that water existed on Mars at one time, so the planet had at least one of the requirements for life.

What was the early history of Mars?

When Mars formed, heavy materials moved toward the center of the planet. Lighter, less dense substances floated to the surface and cooled to form a crust. The hot, molten material underneath pushed through the crust, creating huge volcanoes. These spouted rock, ash, and large amounts of water vapor. The ash spread around the planet and acted as a blanket, slowing the loss

Viking landed on a rock-strewn region of Mars. The rocks appear to have been ejected by violent volcanoes. NASA / HAYDEN PLANETARIUM

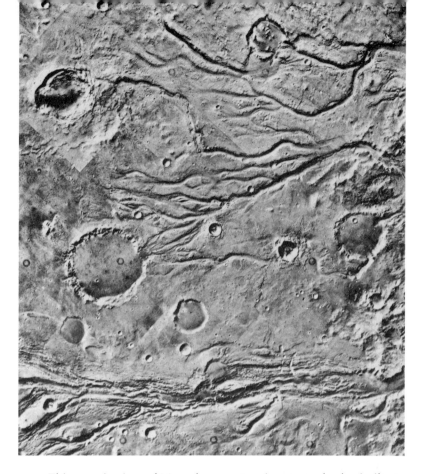

This mosaic view of Mars shows extensive streambeds, similar to those found on Earth. At one time large amounts of water flowed from left to right, cutting a network of valleys that became larger as flow became greater. NASA / HAYDEN PLANETARIUM

of heat from the Martian surface. Water vapor condensed on dust particles in the atmosphere, producing rain. Perhaps rain fell on Mars for millions of years. The water flowed along the surface, cutting channels just as rivers do as they flow over Earth's surface.

Eventually, particles in the ash clouds fell, the volcanoes quieted, and the rains ceased. Mars lost much of its water and atmosphere to space because its gravitation was not strong enough to hold them. Water that did not escape soaked into the surface, making a permafrost, a permanently frozen surface layer, which may still exist. Water also collected at the polar regions, especially the north polar area, where it can still be identified during summer in the northern half of the planet. The only gas left in the atmosphere is carbon dioxide, and there is not much of that. Carbon dioxide is a dense gas and so it would have been the least apt to escape.

What are the canals of Mars?

Centuries ago people wondered about life on Mars. In 1877 there was great excitement, for in that year the Italian astronomer Giovanni Schiaparelli reported that he had seen channels on the planet. The Italian word for channel is *canale*. When people heard that word, they thought of a man-made, or Martian-made, waterway, and so they believed there must be creatures of some kind there. Some years later that belief was strengthened by Percival Lowell, an American astronomer. He reported that the canals made a network, as though they were used for moving things from one place to another, or to supply water to crops. When people heard this, they were convinced there was life on this alien world. Novels such as *War of the Worlds* by H. G. Wells, which describes an invasion of Earth by Martians, fed their appetite. But when the planet is seen more clearly, the canals are found to be illusions produced by the less-than-perfect viewing conditions available to early observers.

Nevertheless, until 1976, when instruments were put on the planet, a good many scientists were sure that life existed on Mars because of those wiggly waterways.

What did Viking probes discover on Mars?

In the summer of 1976, two Viking spacecraft landed on Mars, the first on Chryse Planitia, the Plain of Gold, named for its yellowish color. Each Viking consisted of a landing section that descended to the Martian surface and an orbiter that continued to go around the planet. Information gathered by the landers was sent to the orbiters and, in turn, was relayed to Earth.

Numerous photographs sent to Earth were studied carefully for signs of life, such as small plants, growths on rocks, or movements. At one time it was thought that a rock had been moved from one place to another, but it was an effect caused by shifting shadows. There were no life signs at all.

The Vikings contained robot laboratories controlled by radio signals. The labs were equipped to conduct experiments to discover if there were microbes or bacteria in the Martian soil.

One of the experiments was to examine molecules to see if they contained carbon compounds. Carbon is an element essential to the development of life. Results of the experiment were not conclusive; that is, it was not clear whether or not such compounds had been identified. However, other experiments worked better.

Viking instruments studied the atmosphere, which was found to contain 95 percent carbon dioxide, about 2 percent nitrogen, and 1 percent argon. There were also traces of oxygen, carbon monoxide, neon, krypton, and xenon. Air pressure was very low, only about one-hundredth of the pressure at Earth's surface. There was no water vapor in the atmosphere, except perhaps at the edges of the north polar region. There may be underground ice layers at that location, or simply surface water that is frozen solid most of the time.

To study Martian soil, the Vikings were equipped with soil scoopers. An arm extended out from the probe, scooped up soil, and brought it into the lab for study.

One experiment heated a soil sample enough to drive out any organic material it might contain. The gases given off appeared to be nothing more than carbon dioxide and a small amount of water vapor, both of which could have come from Mars itself and not from plants or animals.

Here on Earth almost any soil sample will contain various kinds of bacteria, yeasts, and molds. These are very hardy organisms, and so the labs on the Vikings looked for them in the Martian soil. Samples of soil were placed in a nutrient solution, one that contained food for microorganisms. If they were present, the organisms would take up the nutrients and convert part of them into gases such as methane, nitrogen, hydrogen, and hydrogen sulfide. The test was conducted for seven months, during which time the sample was kept at an even temperature.

Only carbon dioxide and oxygen were identified. Both gases appeared very quickly, and then production fell off rapidly. This made observers conclude that the gases were simply driven out of the soil, and were not produced by anything in the soil itself.

Experiments using radioactive tracers, or radioactive atoms, to follow movements of atoms from a nutrient solution into an organism, and then released by the organism, produced similar results.

In another experiment Martian soil was sealed inside a chamber that was brightly lighted, as if by the Sun. After several hours, gases given off by the soil were studied to see if organic compounds had been formed. As before, results were disappointing. In spite of the lack of evidence, some scientists still believe there is life on Mars. They say that we have explored only two locations and cannot be certain. All that is necessary is to look in the right places, they insist, and signs of Martian life will be found.

Most observers feel otherwise. They agree that the gases necessary for life are present on Mars, though in very small amounts. There is water, also, but not very much. Other conditions, however, are not favorable for organisms—the lack of water vapor, extremes of temperature, and lack of lasting bodies of liquid water. The possibility that Mars has life on it now, or ever supported life, is very slim. But many still contend that we know very little about the planet. When we are able to explore the entire Martian surface, they think we'll find that Mars once was a living planet.

Have pieces of Mars fallen on Earth?

A few years ago geologists discovered meteorites at Allan Hills and Elephant Moraine in Earth's antarctic ice sheet. Study of them revealed that they contain isotopes of argon and xenon that closely resemble the isotopes that were identified on Mars by the Viking probes. Isotopes are atoms that vary in the number of neutrons they contain. For example, all argon atoms contain 18 protons, and most contain 22 neutrons. Some of the atoms may contain more or fewer neutrons; they are argon isotopes.

Scientists believe that the meteorites were subjected to large shocks about 180 million years ago. Very likely they were ejected from Mars at that time, when very large objects such as asteroids crashed into the Martian surface. The impact could have been great enough to cause a colossal explosion that accelerated particles to speeds great enough for them to escape from the gravity of Mars. The freed particles went into Sun-circling orbits, and some apparently were captured by Earth's gravitation.

The antarctic meteorites will be studied to learn more about them. Expeditions will search for more of them in the antarctic ice sheets. The mystery of the Martian pieces is one that will occupy scientists for many years.

PLUTO AND CHARON

Where is Pluto?

It takes about 8½ minutes for light to travel from the Sun to Earth. Pluto is so much farther away that it takes sunlight more than 5½ hours to reach it. Pluto is forty times farther from the Sun than we are. By the time sunlight reaches Pluto, it has lost much of its intensity, making the planet very cold—some 230°C below zero. That is not much above −273°C, the coldest anything can get.

Most of the time, Pluto is the outermost planet. But until 1999, it is closer to the Sun than Neptune. Pluto's orbit is a flat ellipse that causes its distance from the Sun to range from 4.4 to 7.4 billion kilometers. Presently it is located close to where it gets nearest to the Sun, while Neptune is at its greatest distance from the Sun—4.5 billion kilometers away.

Pluto is an outer planet, but it is different from Jupiter, Saturn, Uranus, and Neptune, the other outer planets. They are all very large and are composed mostly of gases. Pluto is small, the smallest of all the planets, and it appears to contain little, if any, gaseous material. The surface may be made of solid, frozen methane.

Why should the planet be so small? Why should it have a satellite? Is it really a planet? These are some of the riddles of Pluto.

Is Pluto a planet?

Because it is so small, some astronomers have suggested that Pluto is not a planet. Rather, they believe that at one time it was a satellite of Neptune. At some time long past, a star may have come in close to the Sun and disturbed the orbits of established planets and satellites. There may have been a tug of war between the star and Neptune. The star won when it pulled away from Neptune's outermost satellite and put it into a new orbit. Pluto is that satellite. Or two Neptunian satellites may have been affected. These are Pluto and Charon, the satellite that moves around Pluto.

According to the Nemesis Hypothesis, such a star visit occurs every 26 to 30 million years. This theory says that one of five thousand or so candidate stars, we don't know which one, is a companion to the Sun. It is being called the Nemesis star, after the mythological goddess concerned with punishment. The Sun and the Nemesis star go around each another and, every 26 to 30 million years, come closer together. According to the theory, that is what happened 65 million years ago, when the dinosaurs disappeared from Earth. That same visit, or one that occurred millions of years or more earlier, may have been the event that produced Pluto and Charon.

Some people have suggested that it was not a star that pulled Pluto away from Neptune. They say that it was a planet, planet number ten of the solar system. The planet, they say, is out beyond Pluto, so far away that it has escaped detection. To date no such planet has been found.

Perhaps, as others contend, Pluto and Charon are small chunks of matter that formed at the time the other planets came into existence. Pluto may be leftover material.

Whether or not Pluto is a planet depends upon how planet is defined. Some say a planet must move in a solar orbit. Pluto does, so from that standpoint it is a planet. But asteroids and comets also move in a solar orbit, so other standards must be used. One of them might be size.

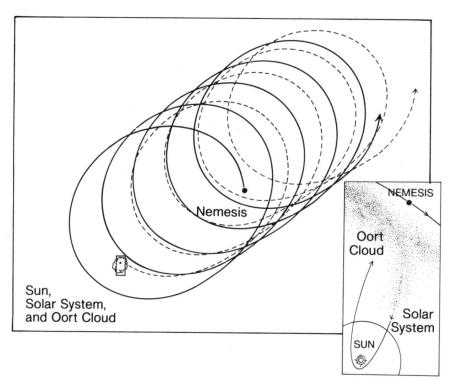

Sun,
Solar System,
and Oort Cloud

NEMESIS

Oort
Cloud

Solar
System

SUN

According to the Nemesis Hypothesis, the Sun has a companion—the Nemesis star—and the two move around each other. Every 26 to 30 million years, the two come closer together. When they do, the Nemesis star pulls particles out of the Oort cloud, which surrounds our solar system. Earth then traps these particles, and they form a blanket around the planet, preventing sunlight from reaching the surface. The resulting cold spell lasts several years and destroys many plants and animals. (Inset at right not drawn to scale)

What is the size of Pluto?

Pluto is very small, only 3000 kilometers in diameter, and it has very little mass, only about one five-hundredth as much as that of Earth. Is that enough to be called a planet? Some people think not. Pluto also has low density, less than that of water. We do not know what it is made of, though probably it is largely methane.

Charon, the satellite of Pluto, is just as much of a puzzle. It is 1200 kilometers in diameter, which is small. Yet it is large to be a satellite of Pluto. The planet's diameter is only two and a half times that of Charon. The two are so alike in size that they are often thought of as a double planet, two planets that are moving around one another. The gravitational pull of each on the other is enough to cause them to have the same surface toward each other all the time. If you were on Pluto and Charon happened to be above your location, it would always be there—and the same face of Charon would always be turned toward you.

In 1999, Pluto will move out beyond Neptune's orbit. Once again the tiny planet will be the outermost object of the solar system. Because of its great distance from Earth, it will remain elusive. Is it a planet or an escaped satellite, or is it debris left over from planet formation? The mysteries are far from being solved.

9 LIFE ON THE PLANETS

No sign of life was found on the Moon by astronauts who explored it. Probes that have landed on Mars, Mercury, and Venus have also disclosed not the slightest indication of life. So far as we know, there is nothing alive on any of the other planets. Earth is the only planet that supports life.

What is the main requirement for life?

In trying to solve the mystery of why life appeared only on our planet, scientists compare it with the others to see how Earth is different.

Very likely, early forms of life had to develop in water. To support life a planet must have large amounts of water, and the water must be liquid; it cannot be frozen continually. It is possible to exist without oceans of water. But life cannot develop or flourish without an abundant supply. Of all the planets, Earth is the only one that contains large amounts of water.

Earth is the life planet, and it is also the water planet. It seems that Earth's large amount of liquid water is the main reason it supports life.

How does temperature affect life?

Certain bacteria can survive in hot springs where the temperature is above boiling, while others can live through centuries of ice-cold temperatures. But most of the plants and animals on Earth must live within a temperature zone between 10° and 50°C. This is a range of only 40 degrees.

If you were out in space measuring Earth's average temperature, as an entire planet it would be 14°C, or very close to it. That temperature has held for the past several millenniums. Earth has existed for some 4.5 billion years, and during that time there have been many temperature changes. Some of them were large enough to cause disasters on the planet. For example, it is believed that a cold spell during which the average temperature dropped several degrees occurred some 65 million years ago. It lasted several decades and brought about the extinction of the dinosaurs. The drop in temperature may have been caused by a cloud of dust that blocked out sunlight. The dust may have been pulled out of the Oort cloud, the dust cloud that surrounds the solar system. Gravitation of a star that is a companion to the Sun, the Nemesis star, could have caused the disruption.

Although temperatures have varied during Earth's history, there have also been periods of several million years when the temperature has remained fairly even. An even temperature existing for millions of years is probably a condition essential to the formation of organic cells, and to the evolution of those basic cells of life into organisms.

What kind of atmosphere does life require?

Living cells contain a great many materials. The main ones are carbon, hydrogen, oxygen, and nitrogen. And these are also the basic ingredients of food: Proteins contain all four of them, and carbohydrates contain the first three. Earth's atmosphere contains all of them.

The kinds of gases in the atmosphere are important to the appearance of life. So also are the amounts of gases and the pressure of the atmosphere. Very high pressure would cause collapse of a growing organism. Low pressure would disrupt its intake of gases and nutrients. A moderate pressure, and one that remains essentially the same through long periods of time, appears to be a requirement for life to develop. Only on our own planet has such a condition existed.

Only Earth has an atmosphere of nitrogen, oxygen, small amounts of carbon dioxide, hydrogen, and the rare gases argon, neon, and xenon. Oxygen is the gas of life; plants and animals breathe it. Nitrogen is the source of nitrates, which plants need in order to thrive. And they need carbon dioxide for photosynthesis, their food-making process.

How has Earth's atmosphere changed?

During Earth's history the atmosphere has gone through many changes. At one time it probably contained large amounts of methane and ammonia, just as the major planets do now. These materials, and others on the early Earth, were inorganic. That is, they were not living, and could in no way ever become organic by themselves. However, severe lightning or waves of high energy from the Sun may have discharged in mixtures of methane, ammonia, water, and hydrogen. If so, amino acids might have been formed. These are substances that occur in proteins and in living organisms. Some scientists believe that such amino acids might have washed into the sea, where the molecules combined. Over long periods of time, and in the proper surroundings of temperature and food, the amino acids might have formed into living cells, the basic structure of life.

Once produced, the amino acids were not destroyed because temperature, pressure, food, and water were favorable. Could it be that Earth is the only place in the universe where such conditions have existed?

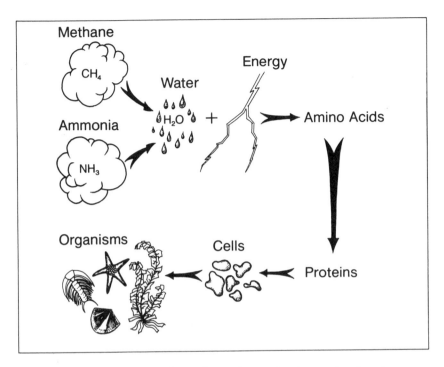

Simple amino acids have been formed when scientists have bombarded steam (water), methane, and ammonia with 60 000 volts of electricity. The same reaction may have occurred billions of years ago on Earth. The amino acids may have washed into the seas and combined to create complex molecules and small organisms.

Could there be life on Jupiter?

Some people suggest that Jupiter is a likely location for life. Beneath the hydrogen-helium atmosphere of the planet there are layers of methane and ammonia. And there are trace amounts of many other substances, including water. At the distance of Jupiter, solar energy is less intense. But Voyager probes have discovered that the planet is bombarded constantly by severe lightning discharges.

These conditions have led many observers to believe that

amino acids are being created on Jupiter. Some people then take the next step, saying that if there are amino acids, then life may soon emerge on Jupiter, if it has not already.

Perhaps they are right, but it is not very likely. The oceans on Jupiter, if they do exist, are oceans of hydrogen under high pressure, not oceans of water. But, these people suggest, life may have adapted to the clouds of Jupiter, where there is some water. Temperatures in the lower portions of the clouds, however, are much too high for the molecules to survive.

Eventually conditions on Jupiter may modify somewhat. Its temperature may moderate and level off, pressure may decrease, and it may then become a cradle of life. On the other hand, the temperature may rise abruptly. Jupiter may gather in enough mass from asteroids and comets to become a star. No one can say.

Conditions on the other major planets are in many ways similar to those on Jupiter. There are people who believe that even if life should never appear on Jupiter, it may evolve on Saturn, Uranus, or Neptune. It may also develop on Titan, one of Saturn's satellites.

Could there be life on Titan?

Saturn has seventeen satellites that are recognized, and there may be more. The largest is Titan, with a diameter of 5150 kilometers, making it bigger than Pluto or Mercury. The satellite has an atmosphere, mostly of methane, and its thickness is about the same as that of Earth. But it is cold there, at least −200°C.

Nevertheless, of all the satellites, Titan is the only one where life could possibly emerge. Beneath the atmosphere, temperatures are probably higher, but chances are they would not reach much above the coldest temperatures on Earth. That is too cold for living things as we know them to prosper.

If Titan has any water, and it probably does, the water would be frozen. Instead of lakes of water, Titan may have methane lakes. Suggestions that life may somehow originate in methane ponds have been made. But most biologists think that is most unlikely.

Titan may be an active satellite, one where there are many volcanic eruptions. The volcanoes may eject water and other gases that could gradually change Titan's atmosphere. Conditions on the satellite might eventually change enough for carbon, hydrogen, oxygen, and nitrogen to be combined into amino acids.

Although a considerable part of the solar system has been explored, our knowledge of it is limited. However, as far as we have learned, Earth is the only location in the solar system where life exists. Why it should be here and nowhere else has been an everlasting mystery.

Could there be life beyond Earth?

Could it be that, in the entire universe, life is limited to our planet? Or are there other planets that support life out among the stars of our galaxy, or in galaxies far beyond our own? This is a great mystery.

A few people have concluded that we are the only creatures of high intelligence in the universe, and some even say that Earth is the only place where there is life of any kind. However, a large number feel that the universe is so large that there must be other places where the conditions necessary for the emergence of life have existed or do exist. In our own galaxy there are some 200 billion stars. A good many of those stars seem to be accompanied by companions having lower mass. These companions may be planets.

Beyond our galaxy there are other galaxies. No doubt there are billions of them, and each of those galaxies is made of billions of stars. Among those billions upon billions of stars there are millions, and perhaps billions, that may have planets. It hardly seems possible that none of these planets ever has had the temperature, pressure, chemicals, and energy believed necessary for life to begin.

Such ideas are only conjecture. No clues to the mystery of life beyond Earth have ever been uncovered. We have never seen another planet beyond our solar system, nor have we picked up a radio signal that might have originated on such a planet. But, as many people say, that does not prove there are no planets out there. Nor does it prove that, should there be planets, they do not contain intelligent creatures.

Does Vega have planets?

The constellation Lyra rides high in the summer skies. It is notable because it contains the bright star Vega. Together with Altair and Deneb, Vega makes up what is called the summer triangle. Vega is a young star, about a billion years old, and it is twice the size of the Sun. It is 26 light-years away—its light takes 26 years to reach us.

In 1983, the Infrared Astronomy Satellite, IRAS, discovered that Vega is surrounded by a cloud of small, cool, solid objects. Possibly it is a solar system or one that is in the process of formation. All the particles appear to be very small; however, some astronomers suspect there may also be larger ones not yet detected.

We may be observing a planet system in the process of forming, much the same as ours was a few billion years ago. If this is true, the discovery is especially exciting, for it is proof that our theories of planet formation are correct. Also, if a planet system is now forming around Vega, a young star, it seems reasonable to expect that systems have also developed around other, older stars. Perhaps some of them are as old as Earth. If so, it is possible that life of some kind evolved on those planets, much as it did on our own.

The IRAS discovery of the cloud surrounding Vega may be one

IRAS has revealed that some forty stars, among them the young star Vega in the constellation Lyra, are surrounded by clouds of cool particles. These may be the materials out of which planets will eventually form.

of the great discoveries of the twentieth century. Along with that discovery, there were observations of other interesting formations.

One of them appears to be a huge disk of small particles that extends 60 billion kilometers beyond the star Beta Pictoris in Pictor, a small, dim constellation in the southern skies, near Canopus, a bright star. Seen almost edge-on, the disk is very thin. Also, Beta Pictoris can be seen through the disk, indicating that there are gaps in it. In those places, particles may have been swept together to make larger masses, either separate planets or, since there are many gaps, an entire planet system.

Mysteries abound in our solar system, in our galaxy, and also in formations far beyond our own. Science is the never-ending adventure that seeks to explore and find solutions to these mysteries.

FURTHER READING

Branley, Franklyn M. *Jupiter: King of the Gods, Giant of the Planets.* New York: Lodestar Books, 1981.

————. *The Nine Planets.* New York: Thomas Y. Crowell, 1978.

————. *Saturn: The Spectacular Planet.* New York: Thomas Y. Crowell, 1983.

Moore, Patrick, and Hunt, Garry, eds. *The Moon* (Rand McNally Library of Astronomical Atlases for Amateur and Professional Photographers). New York: Rand McNally, 1981.

INDEX

Page numbers in *italics* refer to captions.

space probes:
  to Jupiter, 24, 51
  to Mars, 15–17, *38,* 40–42
  to Uranus, 28
  to Venus, 15–17, 23, 48
starlight, dimming of, 30
stars, 54, 56
  brown dwarf, 10
  evolution of, 14
  formation of, 8, 35–36
  mass of, 8, 10
  nuclear fusion of, 10, 36
  number of, 53
  temperature of, 35–36
star systems, 8
storms:
  on Earth, 31, 33
  on Jupiter, 31, *32,* 33–35,
    34
sulfur, 28, 33
sulfur dust, 28
summer triangle, 54
Sun, 8, *9*
  age and life span of, 14
  companion star of, 45, *46,*
    49
  energy radiations from,
    19–20, *20,* 22–23, *22*
  expansion of, 14
  mass of, 12
  movements of, 12, *13*
  planets' distance from, 3, 7

telescopes, 24
  ground-based, 8, 10
Tempel, Ernst W., 31
temperatures:
  absolute zero, 20
  of Earth, 20
  of Jupiter, 33
  of Mars, 23

temperatures, *cont'd*
  of Mercury, 21
  of Neptune, 21
  of planets, 19–23, *22,* 29,
    33, 44
  of Pluto, 44
  of Saturn, 20–21
  support of life and, 37, 42,
    46, 49, 52
  of Uranus, 21, 29
  of Venus, 21–23, *22*
theory of relativity, 4
tides, 11–12
Titan, life formation on, 52–53
Tombaugh, Clyde, 4

Uranus, 3
  atmosphere of, 28
  axis of, 29
  as gaseous, 6–17, 18
  heat sources from, 29
  information chart about, *6–7*
  magnetic poles of, 29
  magnetism of, 18, 29
  rings of, *25,* 26, 28
  rotation of, 18
  satellites of, 28
  temperature condition on,
    21, 29

Van Biesbroeck 8 (VB8), 10
Vega, 8
  cloud surrounding, 8, 54–56,
    55
Venus:
  atmosphere of, 5, 21–23, *22*
  atmospheric pressure on, 23
  information chart about, *6–7*
  life on, 48
  magnetism of, 15–16
  rotation of, 11–12, 17

ABOUT THE AUTHOR

Franklyn M. Branley is the popular author of more than 125 books for young people about astronomy and other sciences. His books include *Halley: Comet 1986, Space Colony, Jupiter,* and four other books in the Mysteries of the Universe Series.

Dr. Branley is Astronomer Emeritus and former chairman of The American Museum–Hayden Planetarium. He and his wife live in Sag Harbor, New York.

ABOUT THE ILLUSTRATOR

Sally J. Bensusen is a science illustrator. Her work appears in the other books in the Mysteries of the Universe Series and in *Halley: Comet 1986.* She has done illustrations for the Smithsonian as well as for many science magazines. She lives in Washington, D.C.